M I N I A T U R E   R O S E S

M I N I A T U R E   R O S E S

by rayford clayton reddell

photographs by saxon holt

CHRONICLE BOOKS
SAN FRANCISCO

Library of Congress Cataloging-in-Publication Data.
Reddell, Rayford Clayton.
Miniature roses / by Rayford Clayton Reddell; photographs by Saxon Holt.
p.   cm.   Includes index.   ISBN 0-8118-1844-6 (hardcover)
1. Miniature Roses. 2. Miniature Roses—Pictorial works.
I. Holt, Saxon. II. Title.   SB411.65.M55R44   1998   635.9'33734—dc21   97-30393 CIP

Printed in Hong Kong

Cover and book design by Gregory Design, San Francisco

The photographer wishes to thank Ann Leyhe for scouting and styling assistance;
additional styling assistance Devora Nussenbaum of Verdure, Barbra Friedman of
Bennett Valley Farm, and Lisa Ledson. Thanks to those gardeners who grew the roses:
Garden Valley Ranch, Rose Gilardi, Ralph Moore, Michael Fischer of Michael's Roses,
Katie Trefethen, Linda Prater, Kay Woods, June Sheppard.

Distributed in Canada by Raincoast Books
8680 Cambie Street
Vancouver, B.C. V6P 6M9

10   9   8   7   6   5   4   3   2

Chronicle Books
85 Second Street
San Francisco, CA 94105
Web Site: www.chronbooks.com

This book is dedicated to Ned Wales,

with appreciation

for his convincing me to take a hard second look

at Miniature Roses.

T A B L E   O F   C O N T E N T S

INTRODUCTION

I grew up in Louisiana with a mother who absolutely refused to admit roses to her garden. "Roses are flat out too much trouble," she used to declare as she devoted time to her azaleas and camellias, grumbling about the fact that roses have more diseases and ailments named specifically for them than does any other flower.

As an adult, I chose to ignore Mother's warnings and proceeded to fall head over heels in love with roses. When I could cram no more in my San Francisco garden, I went commercial and began growing garden roses for the sale of their blossoms.

In fairness, I must concede that Mother was correct—roses are a lot of trouble. I'm equally adamant, however, that they're worth the bother. But never mind—those are the woes of growing full-size rosebushes. Miniature roses are quite another matter.

Minis (as they're commonly called today) are so much less needful than their larger relatives that they should almost be thought of as another flower. As you'll see from the various aspects of growing them, Minis don't persistently beckon diseases, aren't fussy about how they're handled as cut flowers, and are so relatively indifferent to pruning that many people take hedge clippers to them.

Finally, few flowering plants take so beautifully to container culture as Miniature roses do. People who haven't the luxury of garden space can grow them well in pots on sundecks, patios, even fire escapes. And, of course, blossoms can be enjoyed either as cut flowers or when left on plants that can be brought indoors when in bloom.

All in all, Minis are a thorough delight, and their irresistible hell-bent-for-survival habits are what I want to concentrate on in this little book. If the Miniature rose varieties I suggest you consider had been available when my mother was alive, I'll bet she'd have fallen for them, too—Minis are hardly any bother at all.

1

H I S T O R Y

Considering how insanely popular Miniature roses are today, it's easy to imagine that they've been with
us since roses were first grown. In fact, the history of the Miniature rose prior to the beginning of the 19th
century is shrouded in mystery.

Probably because so many roses trace their roots to China, authorities agree it's likely
that the first Miniature roses grew there and that they were a happy coincidence to growing
Rosa chinensis, a highly "variable" species rose native to China. Variable roses are those that
frequently change their growth habits—conventional shrubs often mutate to climbers or ground
covers, or radically alter the overall size of their plants and/or blossoms. It would be convenient
if such a miniature mutation had been botanically identified as *R. chinensis minima*, but none
actually was.

How Miniature roses got to Europe is also unknown, but botanical sketches prove
that they arrived sometime in the 19th century and that they enjoyed moderate popularity in
both England and France. Then in 1918 an officer in the Swiss army medical corps named
Roulet spotted Miniature roses growing as pot plants in an Alpine village and told his friend

'little artist'

Henry Correvon, an avid horticulturist from Geneva, about his find. What excited the two men was that the plants grew only 2 inches tall and produced an abundance of tiny pink blossoms for most of the year.

Correvon obtained cuttings and built a stock of the rose that he introduced to commerce in 1922 as *R. rouletii*, in honor of his friend. In the process he made another discovery—that the rose grew taller than a mere 2 inches when it was cultivated outdoors as a garden plant, rather than confined to a pot.

More than a decade elapsed before anything else happened to foster the development of Miniature roses. Then Jan de Vink, a Dutch breeder in the famous nursery district of Boskoop, decided to experiment with *R. rouletii* by crossing it with dwarf Polyantha roses popular at the time. Although de Vink didn't realize it then, history would prove that he hit the jackpot when he crossed *R. rouletii* with 'Gloria Mundi' to produce a tiny plant that blossomed in red flowers with a white eye. He named his offspring 'Peon' and introduced it to commerce. It attracted little attention until the pioneering American rosarian Robert Pyle of Pennsylvania's Conard-Pyle rose nursery spotted it and realized its potential.

Pyle had little doubt of the marketability of 'Peon', but he thought that a catchier name was needed. In 1936 the rose was renamed 'Tom Thumb' and the rest is history; the Miniature rose was off and running. Young Tom was such an immediate hit that after its first year in commerce, it had to be withdrawn from the Conard-Pyle catalog for a year so the

'tom thumb'

company could build up stock to meet the demand. Another plus came when hybridizers learned that young Tom was a prodigious stud rose with exceptionally fertile pollen. In short time, scads of Miniature roses were bred for market.

Early hybridizing efforts were made primarily in Europe. Besides de Vink's continuing efforts, Pedro Dot of Spain, Meilland of France, and Tauntau of Germany all introduced Miniature roses that are still in commerce. Then the scene switched to the United States.

Because of his extensive work with Miniature roses, Ralph Moore of Visalia, California, has earned the nickname "the father of modern Miniature roses." Although Moore began his hybridizing efforts with the same varieties used in Europe (including *R. rouletii*), he was fascinated by the potential of the Miniature rose and saw no reason why Mini varieties shouldn't blossom in a wide array of colors or have mossing, stripes, and classic form; neither could he fathom why they couldn't be bred to climb or grow prostrate. In a career spanning more than 60 years (he turned 90 in 1996), Moore hybridized more than 300 separate Miniature roses, many of which are the most popular in commerce today.

Once Minis caught on, they spread like gossip, to the point that their introductions today outnumber those of full-size roses. Even though critics point out that the original concept has been lost (that plants remain small enough to fit under a teacup), it's clear that Miniature roses have carved out a permanent spot in rosedom. They're here to stay.

ralph moore's test greenhouse

2

B U Y I N G

In chapter 8, I suggest the Miniature roses I'd grow if I were you, but there are three other fine ways of steering yourself toward good Minis.

First, the American Rose Society identifies good roses of all types, including Miniatures, in its annual publication *Handbook for Selecting Roses*. From tabulations of scores assigned by voting members of the ARS, rose varieties·are given a numerical assignment on a scale of 1.0 to 10.0 (the higher the score, the better the rose). For the most part, you shouldn't consider rose varieties with a score lower than 7.0 (the lower end of roses deemed "good"). The *Handbook* can be had by sending $5 (which includes postage) and a self-addressed, business-size envelope to the American Rose Society, Box 30000, Shreveport, LA 71130-0030.

Second, since 1975, star-performing Miniature roses have been recognized annually through an Awards of Excellence program. Under the auspices of the American Rose Society, test gardens have been established that are dedicated exclusively to the evaluation of newly introduced Minis.

a test garden

I heartily support the establishment of such test centers. My sole concern with the Awards of Excellence program is that it presently includes only six official test sites (they are, however, located strategically for diverse geographic representation). Although I don't think highly of some past winners, a good number of Minis awarded in the Excellence program also made my list of recommendations in chapter 8. A complete list of winners appears in Appendix A.

Third, the considerably more prestigious All-America Rose Selections also operates test gardens in search of roses worthy of the All-America crown. Unfortunately, Miniature roses have been eligible for competition only since 1987, and to date only three varieties have walked away with the award—'Debut', 'New Beginning', and 'Child's Play' (all profiled in chapter 8).

sources

Miniature roses are readily available from a variety of sources, including nurseries and garden centers. Minis are also offered in most rose catalogs, but the widest array of choices can be had from suppliers devoted exclusively to Miniature roses who ship them year-round. A list of such sources is given in Appendix B.

the glories of own-root roses

Of all the many advantages Minis have over their full-size relatives, none is more important than the fact that they grow on their own roots. Before you can appreciate the advantage of

'new beginning', 'loving touch'

own-root cultivation, however, you must appreciate budding, the alternative method of propagation and the one still employed for the vast majority of full-size rosebushes.

Roses that are budded are a grafted combination of two separate rose varieties. The "rootstock" is the part underground. It comes from older varieties known not for their blooms, which are usually insignificant, even ugly, but rather for their capacity for massive root development. To this rootstock a graft is made of the rose variety desired to grow above the ground: the hybrid. The globular bulbous landmark that develops at the point where the two varieties are joined is called the bud union.

Although Miniature roses were budded onto rootstock when they were first introduced to commerce, propagators soon realized that many varieties grew perfectly well on their own roots. What's more, they rooted easily as long as the soil was sandy and moist.

Granted, rosebushes growing on their own roots take longer to mature than do those budded onto rootstock, but advocates claim that the wait is worthwhile because own-root plants are free of virus, don't develop sucker growth, and are cold-hardier.

Another plus for own-root roses is that, because they are small, varieties you're not sure you'll take a shine to can be grown in pots before being transplanted into the garden or to a larger container, where they may be expected to flourish for years.

'jean kenneally'

bareroot or in a container?

All roses go dormant in winter when they shed foliage and store energy for next season's growth. During this time, plants may be dug from the ground and transported with no soil around their roots. Once a year, you have the opportunity to buy Miniature rosebushes bareroot.

The advantage of buying plants bareroot is diversity of availability. At no time during the growing season is so much available. Some nurseries offer plants only during bareroot season, choosing not to go to the trouble of potting up plants for later sales. Most mail-order houses offer plants for sale year-round, however—bareroot for a month or so, then potted into soft plastic pop-out containers the rest of the year.

'my sunshine'

3

PLANTING

Although Miniature roses are considerably more tolerant of growing conditions than are their full-size relatives, when it comes to certain basics, they're identical. When planting in the garden, choose sites carefully.

basic site requirements

Roses must have sun. According to most experts, the minimum is five hours per day. If the climate is temperate, full sunlight is preferable. In areas of intense heat, shading will be necessary, as roses suffer when temperatures exceed 100 degrees F. If you must choose between morning or afternoon sun, go for morning sun with shade in the afternoon.

Look for shelter from the wind; it damages both blooms and foliage. Plant near, but not against, fences and garden walls.

Don't plant roses too near trees or large bushes where they will have to compete with other root systems. Rosebushes, even Miniatures, are voracious feeders and don't like sharing their nutrients with neighbors. Since roses are always thirsty, choose growing sites in reasonable proximity to water sources.

'peach fuzz'

Drainage is just as important as water. Although rose roots require steady amounts of water, they don't like to sit in it. Root damage occurs when water can't drain quickly and thoroughly. An easy way to determine if drainage is adequate is to fill a hole with water and see how long it takes to drain. If more than an hour is required, you'll need to improve drainage by digging holes deeper than you otherwise might have and filling them with coarse gravel.

bareroot plants

Bareroot Minis should be planted as soon as possible after delivery, since they dry out quickly. If their new home isn't yet prepared or if planting is delayed due to bad weather, plants should be "heeled in"—nestled into a trench of loose soil.

A good temporary home is a slanting trench large enough to hold plants leaned on their sides and wide enough to allow for sufficient soil to loosely cover exposed roots. The entire affair should be kept on the wet side of moist until the bushes are placed in their permanent homes.

Even if you're ready to plant as soon as plants arrive, it's wise to soak bushes for at least two hours (no longer than overnight) before putting them into the soil. Submerge entire plants in water, not just the roots, and add a small amount of household bleach (about $1/8$ cup per 5 gallons water). Bleach kills any unwanted bacteria or disease spores, and water plumps out wood.

'little paradise'

You've heard, of course, about the smart fellow who said he'd rather plant a two-bit rose in a four-bit hole than vice versa. Corny as it sounds, it couldn't be truer. No plants love their home more than roses do, and they repay you so generously for affording them organically rich, humus-laden soil to liberally spread their roots in.

Any hole you dig to accommodate a rose (of any size) should be refilled primarily with what is known as "good garden soil"—friable (loose rather than compacted), yet spongy and porous. Add to that agreeable loam 30 percent organic material—peat moss, fine redwood or fir bark chips, good garden compost, or alfalfa meal; better yet, a combination thereof.

If you test your soil's pH—which is a good idea, especially if you grow a variety of plants, some of which prefer alkaline soil, others acid—be advised that roses appreciate soil as close to a pH of 6.5 as possible. Should a soil analysis show that your garden's soil is alkaline (pH 7.0 or higher), add peat or sulfur. Conversely, if the pH is acidic (under 6.0), use agricultural lime to adjust the balance and keep the soil sweet.

After digging a hole large enough to accommodate the bareroot plant, form a tepee of soil and place the bush over it. Although roses growing on their own roots don't have bud unions to serve as landmarks for planting heights, there's ample demarcation of where growth meets roots. Unless you live where winter protection is mandatory, place the growth/root juncture at ground level; in cold-winter areas, consult local rosarians for advice on planting depth. Holding the plant in place, gradually refill the hole with soil, patting it down with your

'mother's love'

hands, *not* your feet. When the hole is half filled, water to soak. Once the water has drained, fill the hole bit by bit with the remaining soil and water again.

planting in containers

As long as drainage can be provided for, almost anything that holds soil will make a suitable container for a Miniature rosebush.

The most popular pots are clay or terra cotta; they're also usually the most decorative. Clay pots keep roots warmer in cold weather and cooler in summer. They also absorb moisture easily. On the down side, they often break if tipped over or crack during severe winters.

Plastic pots have advantages, but not enough. Because they're not as porous as clay, plastic pots don't dry out so easily and can tolerate full sun. On the other hand, plastic doesn't weather and looks brand-new right up until the time it splits and must be replaced.

Wooden containers are fine—they have the same advantages as clay (natural heat regulation and good water absorption), and they don't break so easily.

You should never use metal containers, as they conduct heat so readily that roots may burn; besides that, they rust and stain whatever they're sitting on. Likewise, never use a container with a neck narrower than its base; it's impossible to remove plants from such containers without damaging their root balls.

'hot tamale'

Before you even consider planting a Miniature rosebush in a pot, understand that the variety resolutely dictates the size of the container. As you'll learn from the descriptions in chapter 8, today's Miniature rose varieties differ widely in size. The pot must fit the Mini, holding it comfortably without compressing roots. A 4 to 6 inch pot is appropriate for most Minis, especially young plants. Too large a pot can produce oversized bushes with few or no blooms (overfertilizing achieves the same unfortunate result). Just as for most container plants, provision must be made for adequate drainage, best achieved by placing shards or rocks over the holes in the bottoms of containers.

The commercial soil of choice for containerized Minis is generally labeled "sterile potting soil." It alone will produce fine roses, but to ensure even better production, add 1 tablespoon Epsom salts, $1/4$ cup alfalfa meal, and a handful of peat moss to the soil readied for each pot.

Put enough soil into the pot to hold the plant in place, and gradually add the remaining mix. When the pot is half full, fill it with water and let it drain, then fill it again. Gently press the remaining soil to within $1/2$ inch of the rim. Water, allow the pot to drain thoroughly, then water again.

Be forewarned that plants grown in containers will need more regular care than those grown in the ground. More frequent watering is required, since moisture evaporates not only from the soil but also from the sides of containers. More frequent fertilizing is necessary, too, since watering leaches fertilizers. Also, be prepared for the fact that a containerized rose needs occasional repotting into a larger container because of massive root development.

'rainbow's end'

By far the greatest advantage of growing Minis in containers is their movability. Kept in pots, Minis in full bloom can be brought indoors and placed in decorative cachepots. Many gardeners keep a group of potted Minis hidden from general view when they're not in bloom and move them either indoors when the show starts or to a patio or sundeck where they can be viewed up close.

Minis in pots also serve as good garden fillers when other plants suddenly die or become unsightly. As a temporary replacement in a noticeable gap, a Mini (pot and all) can be dropped into place. Or, if you're certain of its suitability there, the plant may be removed from its pot and planted in place.

planting from containers

If you order Miniature roses from suppliers who supply plants year-round, they will usually arrive in 2 ½ inch plastic cubes so pliable that they release their contents, root ball and all, with a slight squeeze. Root balls of leafed-out Miniature rosebushes are also often wrapped in foil, which should be tenderly removed without dislodging the soil around the roots.

Once the plant has been freed from its container, plant it either in a larger container or directly in the garden, following all the guidelines mentioned earlier.

'starina'

Miniature roses are fine choices for bordering beds containing other flowers (large roses, too, of course). Similarly, they work well for lining paths and driveways.

Planting Miniature roses in raised beds is particularly effective. Not only does providing elevation to eye level make it easier to appreciate their beauty, it makes tending them easier, too.

When planting Minis in groups, the distance between plants is, of course, chiefly dependent on the aspirations of each variety. Micro-minis may be spaced only 6 inches apart, while Macro-minis may demand a spacing of 2 feet from each other. Varieties of average sizes are usually spaced from 7 to 12 inches apart.

Patio walls are often constructed to hold soil in hollow spaces along their top edges. Low-growing Mini varieties work well in such nooks, as do varieties that weep or cascade. Just be vigilant about watering and fertilizing.

Minis are also popular additions to rock gardens, particularly those varieties that grow relatively prostrate. When planting a Mini in a rock garden, however, keep in mind that roses appreciate rich soil. While the relatively poor, gritty soil in most rockeries is fine for alpine plants, the areas where roses are expected to flourish must be punched up with new soil rich in humus.

'rise 'n' shine'

If you decide to devote an entire garden bed to Minis, be careful with selections. Ideally, beds should remain one color, although it is often effective to plant a tall variety in the center of the bed and a shorter variety (of another color, perhaps) beneath it. Keep in mind also that if height is desirable, Miniature roses make fine Tree roses (see chapter 7).

If you simply must have several varieties of different colors in one bed, at least try to segregate them, and plant no fewer than three of each.

'child's play'

4

M A I N T A I N I N G

Miniature roses are much easier to maintain than their full-size relatives. True, they fall prey to certain ailments and attract specific insects common to their ancestors, but never to the same degree as full-size rosebushes. Still, if they're expected to flourish and bloom profusely, certain basic needs must be met.

water

Foremost is water. Not only do roses require steady irrigation, they like being watered in certain ways and only just so often.

Except on mornings you're sure are going to be warm, never water roses from overhead; wet foliage spreads a welcome mat for diseases such as powdery mildew.

It's more important to water deeply than to water often. Feeder roots will develop no matter how you water; it's the long roots you need to train. Encourage deep roots by forcing them down in their search for water.

The best watering method, flooding, is easy if you have mulched, raised beds. When beds are flooded, the water spreads nutrients throughout the mulch, benefiting feeder roots.

'debut'

With proper drainage, water reaches levels well below the soil surface, thus encouraging roots to find it.

It's impossible to tell you precisely how often to water, because proper irrigation is strictly local. Where summers are scorchers, rosebushes must be watered frequently (during heat waves plants in pots may require daily watering), as they should when parching winds are prevalent.

fertilizers

Besides being big drinkers, roses like to eat a lot. In response to meals, bushes reward you with bountiful bloom.

I'm strongly in favor of feeding roses heavily, and it's so easy to do these days. Liquid fertilizers with words such as "Start," "Grow," and "Bloom" in their names encourage rosebushes to do precisely that. Following the manufacturer's suggested rates, I apply liquid fertilizers every other week from a month before the first bloom until a month before the last rose of summer. Which fertilizer formulation I use is entirely dependent on the season. In spring, when I want to urge bushes out of the ground, I concentrate on nitrogen (chemical symbol N), the first of the big three elements in the NPK formula of a fertilizer. For the majority of summer, I use "well-balanced" formulations (the three numbers in the NPK formula are equal, such as 10-10-10 or 15-15-15). In fall, when I'm concerned only about the blooms that linger on the bushes, I use no nitrogen at all, only phosphorus (P) and potassium (K) in a

'tiny flame'

formulation such as 0-10-10. You simply can't go wrong with liquid fertilizers; everything you need to know is on their labels.

disbudding

Except for pruning, nothing frightens rose growers more than disbudding. It couldn't be simpler and demands nothing more than a decision whether you prefer rose blossoms one to a stem or in sprays.

If more than one rosebud develops on a stem, one of them (the terminal bud) will be noticeably larger than the others. If you prefer one-to-a-stem blossoms, remove the lesser buds, leaving only the terminal bud to develop on the stem. If you prefer sprays of blossoms on one stem, however, the reverse is true: the terminal bud must be removed so that side buds can develop more fully.

Decide which buds you want to remove before they get longer than $1/4$ inch. At this length, you can grasp them at the base and snap them off close to the stem without leaving a stub.

It's easy to make a disbudding decision when there are three buds developing on a stem—remove the smaller two. Similarly, stems holding five buds are easy to handle—remove the terminal bud and let the side ones develop into a spray. Problems arise, however, when there are four buds on a stem, in which case the choice is entirely yours.

'luis desamero'

diseases

The use of chemical fungicides has always been a subject of heated conversation among rosarians. Owing to the chemicals' toxicity, many gardeners refuse to employ them at all and grow Minis instead of their full-size relatives because of their comparative resistance to the three diseases most common to roses—mildew, rust, and blackspot. If an infestation threatens to get out of hand, organic products such as agricultural soaps or baking soda will often arrest the problem.

While I'll never try to talk someone into using chemicals (although I employ them myself, taking every precaution available), accuracy compels me to mention that chemicals are available today that are safer than ever thought possible. Some are actually less toxic than caffeine or table salt.

Although Miniature roses are considerably more resistant to fungal diseases than are their full-size relatives, they're not immune to insects. Luckily, the most troublesome are easily treated.

Spider mites love Miniature roses for their succulent foliage growing so near to the ground. The only fortunate aspect of spider mites' appearance in most gardens is when they arrive—in the heat of summer, when bushes can safely be thoroughly drenched with water during the day with full expectations of their drying by nightfall. Spider mites detest water, and sprays from water wands will drive them away.

'party girl'

5

H A R V E S T I N G

One of the great pleasures of growing Miniature roses is enjoying them as cut blossoms. To get the longest life from them, learn to harvest blooms at the proper times and to condition them well.

when

Roses begin to draw water up inside their bushes as soon as there's a hint of dusk, and they hold onto all the moisture they can draw into their plants until morning light forces evaporation. Since the blooms that last longest in the vase are those with the highest content of water, always harvest blossoms late in the afternoon or early in the morning. What you most want to avoid is cutting blossoms during the middle of the day, especially when hot weather has rendered blooms limp.

at what stage

Blossoms of all varieties of roses, Minis included, must reach a certain stage of openness before they should be harvested from their mother plant. Otherwise, they won't open further or fully. The rule to follow here is to wait until the sepals are down.

'figurine'

Sepals resemble tiny leaves and completely enclose rosebuds. Although sepals are most usually the same color green as the foliage of the variety on which they grow, they can also have red serrated edges. As rosebuds develop, so do sepals. When they can contain the bloom no longer, they begin to unfurl one by one. When the sepals turn down and the bud is "cracked," as florists describe it, the bloom is ready to be cut.

where

Where a bloom is cut from the bush on which it grows is vital to the plant it leaves behind. Rose foliage comes in sets of leaflets, usually three, five, or seven. Five is the operative number here, but equally important is the precise five-leaflet set above which a cut is made, specifically whether or not it faces outward from the center of the bush. At the base of leaflets and the stems from which they grow is an axil—a swelling red bud that is actually a dormant eye of a rose that will bloom six to eight weeks after the stem above it has been properly cut. Once you've selected a five-leaflet set that faces outward, make a downward sloping cut 1/4 inch above the axil.

conditioning

If you've heeded my advice so far, it would be a shame not to get the longest vase life possible out of your rose blossoms. If you follow this next step, you will.

'sweet chariot' with 'gourmet popcorn'

When flowers with substantial stems such as roses are cut, the stems draw in air. When air reaches the bloom, it causes it to bend over and die prematurely. The remedy to the problem, recutting stems under water, is one of the best-kept secrets in all of rosedom. When I tell people of the wonders of recutting stems under water, they look at me incredulously, and act as though I've ordered them to submerge their flowers (and themselves) in a tub of water and, without benefit of goggles, slice bouquets to smithereens. It's nowhere near so dramatic.

After harvesting blossoms, fill a bowl with fresh water, submerge the tip of each stem 1–2 inches under water, and, with sharp shears, recut $^1/_4$ inch from the bottom of each stem. When stems of roses are recut under water, they draw no air, and the water acts as a temporary sealant when blossoms are later moved around out of water.

If you want to truly gild the lily with blossoms lasting longer than you ever imagined possible, take one more step. Before recutting the stems under water, fill another container with 1 quart of hot water (approximately 105 degrees—usually the hottest water from a kitchen tap), stir in 1 teaspoon of sugar to continue feeding the blossoms once they're off the bush, and add a few drops of household bleach to kill any bacteria.

After recutting all the stems under water and submerging them in the container with the homemade preservative, put the container in the coolest, darkest closet you have until the water reaches room temperature. Blossoms will be turgid and full of substance and can be safely transferred to a vase or bunched for arranging.

'irresistable'

6

P R U N I N G

Before telling you how a lot of experienced gardeners prune their rosebushes these days, I want to tell you about the classics of pruning—why it must be done and how to do it strictly by the book.

Pruning is required for two elementary reasons: to rid bushes of nonproductive, damaged, or dead wood and to shape them. Left unpruned, bushes become tangled masses of spindly wood that selfishly dole out small blossoms. Face it, you have no choice but to prune.

There's a trick to making the task simpler. Two weeks before you intend to prune your rosebushes, strip the plants of all foliage. Once they're stripped of leaves, nature demands that plants rejuvenate themselves and thrust out new growth. The first signs of such growth are swelling bud eyes at the point where a new stem is about to grow—the very landmark necessary for judicious pruning cuts.

Two weeks after stripping, you should then remove wood you *know* must come out—that which is spindly or obviously dead. Once only healthy wood is left, decide how much more you want to remove. With Minis, there are no cardinal rules dictating the precise number of canes that should be left on a plant, nor is there a precise height to which they should be cut back.

'kristen'

How severely you prune your bushes in winter will determine how many blooms you have in spring. *Severe* pruning (necessary in bitter winter climates where winter protection is mandatory) results in fewer blossoms but finer quality. *Light* pruning will yield lots of showy garden displays, usually on flimsy stems. *Moderate* pruning, which calls for canes to be cut back to roughly half their pre-pruned height, is a compromise.

If you have stripped bushes of all foliage two weeks before you intend to prune them, you'll have no difficulty spotting the exact points where cuts should be made—dormant eyes will have swollen and turned red. Look carefully for dormant eyes facing *outward* from the center of the bush, and make pruning cuts approximately 1/4 inch above them.

Once it was believed that cuts had to be made as close as possible to a 45-degree angle. Now such precision is thought to be nothing more than needless busywork. Nevertheless, be careful not to make cuts so close to budding eyes that you run the risk of damaging them or so flat that water might collect and invite disease.

Now the good news. Under the auspices of the Royal National Rose Society (RNRS), British rosarians have been experimenting with unconventional pruning techniques, specifically the use of hedge clippers rather than customary pruning shears. Success with this technique was so encouraging on Miniature roses that experimenters are now testing the approach with conventional full-size bushes. Personally, I'm not yet willing to take hedge trimmers to my Hybrid Tea, Floribunda, or Grandiflora roses, but I'm convinced that Minis can hold up to such seemingly harsh treatment.

'minnie pearl' with other cut roses

In an article written by RNRS secretary Ken Grapes, published in the August 1992 issue of *The American Rose*, British researchers convincingly claim that traditional pruning techniques (locating swelling bud eyes and cutting just above them) were thought necessary because modern roses were once plagued with dieback—the tendency for unproperly cut stems to die back to the spot where a proper cut should have been made. These researchers now say that "rose breeding has come a long way and many modern varieties don't suffer badly from the effects of dieback because they are so much more vigorous." Further, their trials have "showed that rough pruning and hedge trimmer pruning caused no more dieback than traditional pruning."

Leaving themselves an out (just in case their experimentations don't pan out), the British experimenters go on to allow that "it is possible that roses that are roughly pruned may become overcrowded in the center and therefore more prone to diseases. Traditional pruning encourages the development of open-centered bushes. It may therefore be necessary to alternate between rough, or hedge trimmer, pruning and traditional pruning."

I believe the correct approach is indeed a compromise, and I use hedge clippers for the majority of pruning cuts and shears only to open up bushes' centers. It truly works.

'snow bride'

7

S P E C I A L   C U L T I V A T I O N

Both because hybridizers have been intent on breeding Miniature roses that do more than simply grow as bushes and because propagators have been similarly determined to bud Miniature roses into distinguished growth habits, today's Miniature roses have considerable versatility.

Perhaps the most charming of all growth habits of modern Minis is their ability to weep and cascade. Then again, it might be their ability to climb or to cover the ground. As you'll see in the next chapter, varieties are available that do all these things. These characteristics are due to hybridizers' efforts.

Propagators have perfected the art of budding Minis as Standards (Tree roses). Miniature roses grown this way represent the single exception to growing Minis on their own roots, but the exception is a big one because Minis grown as Tree roses aren't merely budded once, they're budded twice. First the hybrid variety is budded onto a bare cane of rosewood to give height to the plant—anywhere from 18 inches to 3 feet tall (even taller if custom budded). Then the bare rose cane is budded at its base onto rootstock, resulting in two bud unions—one on either end of the bare cane of rosewood.

'nozomi' mixed with 'penelope'

Not only are Tree roses popular for Minis that grow as conventional bushes, they're even more so for those that weep. Standards are fine for landscaping and as a means of squeezing in additional roses when your garden has room for roots below but not for bushes above. Since the major growth will be above their neighbors, Tree roses can be planted right between two large bushes. Mini Tree roses are also popular for lining walkways and paths.

Popular, too, are Minis grown in hanging baskets. The very same varieties that perform well as weeping Standards work when grown to cascade from hanging baskets.

Climbing Miniature roses were once rather unambitious in their aspirations to grow vertically. Fortunately, certain modern varieties such as 'Jeanne LaJoie' happily scramble to 10-foot heights. Several others grow less tall but just as vigorously.

As for Ground-Cover Minis, they're just that, aggressively sending out long, relatively prostrate canes. Besides smothering the ground, of course, they, too, can be grown as Standards or in hanging baskets.

'jeanne lajoie'

8

V A R I E T I E S

Before tempting you with varieties of Miniature roses, let me tell you how I've decided to classify them and how honest I'm prepared to be about their qualities.

Dictating the heights that mature plants will reach is, of course, the biggest problem. Rosebushes grow taller where I garden, in Petaluma, California, than they do, say, in Madison, Wisconsin, or Boston, Massachusetts. Conversely, in Santa Barbara, California, varieties reach even greater heights than they do in Petaluma. Still, a standard of reference is required to distinguish Micro-minis (the smallest blooms and plants) from moderate growers, and the latter from the skyscrapers among Minis.

Here's how my coding works: If a variety is categorized as one that grows low to the ground (L), I believe it should remain under 12 inches. Further, I believe that varieties that grow between 12 and 18 inches tall should be classified as medium (M), and hybrids that grow taller than 18 inches should be called tall (T). Special growth habits are designated just as they are—Ground Covers, Climbers, or Weepers. Special attributes such as disease resistance, hardiness, and abundant foliage are also noted.

'loving touch'

As for fragrance, I must admit that I don't grow Miniature roses for their perfume, but that's a touchy subject. Because so many people swear that their Minis are scented, catalog writers seem compelled to mention that certain varieties have "light," "mild," or "slight" fragrance. I beg to differ and believe that these roses aren't actually perfumed, they simply smell fresh—a valuable quality indeed. When I draw attention to a variety's fragrance, I mean that it smells distinctly better than merely fresh. Incidentally, I can't help but notice that the Miniature rose varieties that gardeners agree are the most strongly perfumed are all members of the (T) category. Must a Mini always be tall to harbor perfume in its petals?

The following are varieties I consider worthy of consideration:

'BABY GRAND' produces pure, lightish pink blooms that are winningly formed—whole blossoms segment their petals into quarters, the way many heirloom roses do. Foliage is bright green, and plants are nicely rounded and bushy. Because plants of 'Baby Grand' are of such uniform size, they are especially effective when massed. (M)

'BEAUTY SECRET' is about as pure cardinal red as any Mini in commerce. High-centered blooms are small (1 1/2 inches), and foliage is glossy and leathery. Plants are bushy yet compact and vigorous. 'Beauty Secret' was introduced in 1965, making it an old-timer among Minis. (M)

'BLACK JADE', befitting its name, produces near-black buds that mature into high-centered, elegant dark red blossoms. Bushes are vigorous and stems are exceptionally long. Plants have an agreeable rounded form, and foliage is semiglossy and dark green. (M)

'baby grand'

'CAL POLY' bears intensely yellow flowers that don't fade as they age. Sprays of buds appear more regularly than do one-to-a-stem blossoms, and flowers last particularly well after harvest. Foliage is semiglossy and stems are relatively thornless. Bushes are upright yet bushy. (M)

'CENTER GOLD' blossoms with deep yellow, fully double flowers (up to 60 petals each). Although blooms occasionally occur one to a stem, more frequently they are borne in sprays of up to 12 buds each. Foliage is glossy and thorns are slim prickles that slope downward. Bushes are compact but upright. (T)

'CHEER UP' produces deep orange blossoms that are urn shaped and high centered—pure exhibition form. If blooms don't occur one to a stem (which they usually do), they form in small sprays of three to four blossoms. Foliage is medium size, dark green, and glossy. If fall's last blooms are left on the plants, $1/2$ inch, green-and-brown hips follow. (M)

'CHICKADEE' bears midpink blossoms whose petals are sometimes striped white. While most Minis offer only a whiff of fragrance, 'Chickadee' offers a full-bodied bouquet. Plants are neat and bushy, and flowering is abundant. (M)

'CHILD'S PLAY' was an All-America Rose Selection in 1993 for several reasons, not the least of which is its endearing color scheme—white flowers with broad pink edges. Individual blossoms reach almost 2-inch widths, and plants are vigorous, upright, and bushy. (T)

'cheer up'

'CINDERELLA' is one of Ralph Moore's early Micro-minis. Plants rarely grow taller than 10 inches, and the satiny white flowers never reach beyond 1 inch. Although plants are diminutive, they're upright and their stems carry no thorns. (L)

'CUPCAKE' produces heavily petaled, rounded blossoms that resemble pale pink roses fashioned from cake frosting. Foliage is glossy and plants are vigorous, although they rarely grow taller than 18 inches. (M)

'DEBUT' was selected as an All-America rose in 1989 in large part because of its stunning color combination. Petals of buds to half-open flowers are scarlet with yellow at their bases; as they mature, the scarlet fades to cherry red and the yellow to white. Although most blossoms appear one to a stem, sprays occur, too. Foliage is dark green and semiglossy. Each fall, plants produce a smattering of tiny orange-red hips. (M)

'FAIRHOPE' is a favored Mini among rosarians who exhibit their wares, which is no surprise since blossoms have classic exhibition form and most often appear one to a stem. Color is usually very pale yellow, sometimes almost white. Foliage is medium green and semiglossy, and plants are upright yet bushy. (M)

'FIGURINE' is one of my personal favorites among Minis. If you know the Hybrid Tea 'Pristine' (white edged pink), imagine a miniature version of it and 'Figurine' will fill the bill. Blossoms not only have exhibition form, they come on long cutting stems. Plants are bushy, upright, and vigorous. Fragrance is notable. (T)

'cupcake'

'GOURMET POPCORN' is a sport of 'Popcorn' (also described in this section) and similar in every way but size (it's considerably larger). Plants in full bloom are a sight to behold—masses of tiny fat buds opening into sprays of pure white blossoms that eventually reveal hearts of yellow stamens. When pruned for classic shape, bushes form natural mounds; with less severe pruning, bushes can be trained to weep and cascade, making them naturals for Standards (Tree roses). Foliage is notably resistant to disease. (T)

'HEARTBREAKER' is a dazzling display of colors. Each petal is deep pink at its outer edge, fading gradually to white at its base. Blossoms most often occur in sprays of three to five blooms each, and foliage is small, mahogany red when immature and later dark green, and glossy. Although mature bushes remain rounded, they easily extend to 2 feet tall. (T)

'HOLY TOLEDO' may make you say those very words. Petals are a brilliant color combination—glowing apricot with a yellow-orange reverse. Foliage is small, dark green, and glossy, and plants are vigorous and bushy. (M)

'HOT TAMALE' lives up to its name with blooms that are indeed hot. The insides of the petals are shaded rose-red and the outsides are contrastingly yellow. Blooms most often occur in small clusters and mature into 2 1/2 inch well-formed blossoms. Not only are plants tall, they easily extend to over 2-foot widths. Foliage is dark green and semiglossy. (T)

'IRRESISTIBLE' is just that to exhibitors of Mini roses. Blossom form is superb and color is appealing, too—white with pale pink centers. 'Irresistible' performs in keeping with your disbudding wishes; if you prefer blossoms one to a stem, remove the smaller ones once a

'gourmet popcorn'

terminal bud is obvious (larger than all the others). Otherwise, leave buds alone to develop into sprays of three to five blossoms each. Bushes are large and stems are long. (T)

'JEAN KENNEALLY' is another of my pets among Minis, perhaps because I'm in the business of growing roses for cut flowers and 'Jean Kenneally' has such extended vase life and long stems. Then, too, its true apricot color appeals to everyone. Finally, blossoming is virtually continuous all summer long. (T)

'JEANNE LAJOIE' is delicately colored (pink, tinged coral) but ambitious in growth. Climbing canes easily reach 10 feet tall and, if trained on a trellis, 5 feet wide. Also popular as a Pillar rose, 'Jeanne LaJoie' is notoriously hardy to winter. The disease-resistant foliage is glossy and dark green. (Climber)

'JENNIFER' produces delicate flowers whose porcelain pink petals have a soft white reverse. Medium-size foliage is dark and semiglossy, and plants are bushy with a willing tendency to spread. (T)

'KING TUT' is a newly introduced Climbing mini that produces scads of golden yellow 2-inch flowers with a slight pink tinge. Plants are vigorous to 7-foot heights. (Climber)

'KRISTEN' is a red-and-white bicolor that has a charming habit of opening its blossoms to the half-open stage, then going into a holding pattern. The exhibition-quality blossoms seem to last forever whether left on the plant or cut for a vase. Although blooms most often appear one to a stem, they may occur in sprays of three to five blossoms each. Foliage is large, dark green, and semiglossy. (T)

'jennifer'

'**LITTLE ARTIST**' is a gift from Sam McGredy's efforts to produce his "hand-painted" series of roses, no two blooms of which are exactly alike. The 10–15 petals per bloom are variable shades of red with a white eye surrounding golden yellow stamens. The small, medium green, semiglossy foliage is notably resistant to disease. (M)

'**LITTLE JACKIE**' produces orange-red blossoms with a yellow reverse on each of their 20 petals. Semiglossy foliage is medium size and plants are vigorous. (T)

'**LITTLE PARADISE**' is so named because of its resemblance to the famous Hybrid Tea 'Paradise'. The clusters of exhibition-quality, lavender-tinged-ruby blooms are high centered and shapely. Disease-resistant foliage is dark green and plants are upright. (T)

'**LOVING TOUCH**' certainly deserved its Award of Excellence from the American Rose Society in 1985 for its color alone. Blossoms are rich apricot, deeper in hue where summers are moderate. Blooms usually occur singly, foliage is medium green and semiglossy, and plants are bushy with distinct tendencies to spread. (M)

'**LUIS DESAMERO**' is my personal favorite among yellow Minis because of its appealing pastel coloring. Buds of the 28-petaled blossoms are ovoid but mature into high-centered, exhibition-quality blooms (the rose "shows" well indeed). Flowering includes one-to-a-stem blossoms as well as those formed in clusters of three to five blooms. Medium green foliage is abundant and plants have a graceful spreading habit. (T)

'little jackie'

'LYNNE GOLD' is another of Ralph Moore's triumphant attempts at keeping Minis miniature. Dark to medium gold buds are tiny and open into blossoms only 1 inch wide. In keeping with flower size, foliage is tiny, too. Plants are bushy and spreading but never top 10 inches. (L)

'MAGIC CARROUSEL' has been a favored Mini worldwide since it was introduced in 1972, in large part because of its distinct, crisp coloring. Petals are white edged red, and blossoms are full (to 35 petals each). Another reason 'Magic Carrousel' still enjoys a high rating by voting members of the American Rose Society is that its plants are vigorous and exceptionally easy to grow. In keeping with other outstanding attributes, foliage is small but glossy and leathery. (T)

'MINNIE PEARL' enjoys a 9.5 rating from the American Rose Society (10 is perfect) and it's no wonder. Blossoms are a wondrous combination of pink, coral, and salmon. Buds are pointed, blossoms are shapely, and the plants on which they occur are fully foliated and naturally rounded. Blooms are abundant and colors are best where summers are warm. (T)

'MOTHER'S LOVE' is classified as a pink blend because petals are primarily pink but have yellow at their bases. Flowers are well formed and appear both one to a stem and in clusters. Plants are upright and bushy yet well contained. (M)

'MY SUNSHINE' is a winning yellow Mini mostly because it's single-petaled, but also because its blossoms go through a pleasing color transformation as they age. Young flowers are medium yellow; as blossoms mature, the yellow fades to soft orange and centers of yellow stamens are revealed. Foliage is medium size, medium green, and semiglossy. (T)

'magic carrousel'

'NEW BEGINNING' was selected as All-America in 1989. Although the color of the blossoms isn't for everyone (an eye-blinking combination of orange-red and yellow), no one quibbles with the plant's growth habits (tidy, compact, and symmetrical). Plants carry few thorns and produce no hips. (T)

'NOZOMI' is classified as a Climber, but most people think of it as a Weeper. Because of such natural trailing growth habits, 'Nozomi' is often cultivated as a Ground Cover, even more frequently as a Tree rose. However it's grown, blossoms (always carried in trusses) are single and pearl-pink. Foliage is small and glossy. (Climber)

'PARTY GIRL' is such a popular lass because of the appealing colors of her blossoms— soft apricot slightly tinged salmon-pink. A fine exhibition rose, 'Party Girl' produces high centered shapely buds and blossoms. Plants are upright and vigorous yet well contained. (M)

'PEACH FUZZ' acquired its name in part because its buds are covered in soft moss. Peachy, too, is the color combination in the blooms—apricot and pink. Blossoms, which occur both one to a stem and in clusters of as many as seven flowers each, are well formed and appear at a steady rate all season long. Plants are rounded and bushy. (T)

'PINSTRIPE' blossoms with flowers madly striped red and white, no two exactly alike. Flowers of 35 petals each open fully to reveal golden yellow stamens. Foliage is small, medium green, and semiglossy. Plants are relatively low growing and have natural mounding habits, making 'Pinstripe' a fine Mini to grow as a Tree rose. (M)

'pinstripe'

'POPCORN' is the rose from which 'Gourmet Popcorn' (see previous listing) sported and is similar in all ways except size (it's considerably smaller). Semidouble blossoms with 13 petals each are creamy white and surround bright yellow centers. When the bushes come a cropper (bloom all at once), which they often do, it looks as though someone has tossed a batch of freshly popped corn onto a tough little green bush. (M)

'RAINBOW'S END' is highly rated by the American Rose Society and with good reason. Among other qualities, blooms are an exhibitor's dream—classic Hybrid Tea form and appearing one to a stem more often than in clusters. Blossoms are lemon yellow with scarlet-edged petals. Plants are shapely but vigorous and compact. (M)

'RALPH'S CREEPER' is proof positive of Ralph Moore's determination to hybridize Minis that do more than grow as conventional bushes. This Ground Cover spreads to over 5-foot widths but never grows taller than 24 inches (more usually, 18). Blossoms, which are vibrant red with a yellow eye, are borne in sprays of 10–15 flowers each. Not only does 'Ralph's Creeper' gobble up whole hillsides when planted in masses, it also tolerates more than a fair share of shade. (Ground Cover)

'RED CASCADE' is officially classified as a Climber, but it's better grown as a Ground Cover. Individual deep red flowers are small (to 1 inch wide), but they literally shower the plants and repeat well. Cultivated as a Ground Cover, plants extend to over 5 feet. 'Red Cascade' makes a fine Mini for a hanging basket (it also grows well as a Standard). (Ground Cover)

'ralph's creeper'

'RING OF FIRE' is a favorite among gardeners who grow Minis for cut flowers because blossoms enjoy an extended vase life. Blooms literally glow with color—yellow edged red, the overall effect of which is orange. Plants are bushy, upright, and vigorous. (T)

'RISE 'N' SHINE' is highly thought of both by members of the American Rose Society, who gave it an 8.8 rating, and by its hybridizer, Ralph Moore, who considers it his best yellow. Flowers are rich medium yellow, buds are long and high centered, and half-open flowers are exceptionally shapely. Plants are bushy and upright. (T)

'ROCKETEER' hasn't been around long enough for anyone to be certain how high it will climb, but I'm sure it's to at least 5 feet. The bright coral-orange flowers are large for a Mini (to 2 inches across), but so is the bright midgreen, glossy foliage. Flowers open fully to reveal clusters of bright yellow stamens and a yellow eye. (Climber)

'RUBY PENDANT' is registered as mauve, but its colors actually include reddish purple. Exhibitors treasure it because its buds and blossoms are high centered and shapely and almost always appear one to a stem. Foliage is a distinctive reddish green and plants are vigorous. (T)

'SCENTSATIONAL' is a recently introduced Mini whose fragrance is no pretense— blossoms are packed with perfume. Prized as cut flowers (usually one bloom per stem), blossoms are mauve edged pink, with a creamy petal reverse. Buds are urn shaped and maintain their fine form through maturity. (T)

'ring of fire'

'**SEQUOIA GOLD**' produces medium yellow buds that fade to light yellow blossoms, occurring both one to a stem and in clusters of as many as seven blooms. Flowering is profuse, and plants are vigorous and spreading (often growing as wide as they are tall). (M)

'**SI**' is a Micro-mini from the hybridizing hands of Spain's Pedro Dot. A conversation piece, the rosy white buds of 'Si' are approximately the size of a grain of wheat, and plants rarely get taller than 9 inches. (L)

'**SNOW BRIDE**' is a creamy white Mini that's as at home in the garden as it is on the exhibitor's table. Plants have deep green foliage and a natural habit of forming compact mounds. Flower form is best where summers are moderate. (M)

'**SPICE DROP**' is a Micro-mini whose blossoms are both delicate and well formed. Salmon-pink flowers shower the small plants throughout the blooming season, and the ample foliage is dark green. Mature plants may hover at 6 inches or extend to 8. (L)

'**STARINA**' was once the highest-rated Miniature rose in commerce. Although it's still highly thought of, its rating has dropped (probably because its near-garish orange-red color doesn't wear well on the eyes). Still, the pointed buds and shapely flowers are admirable, and plants sport glossy dark green leaves. (M)

'**SWEET CHARIOT**' produces purple buds that gracefully fade to lavender as they mature and open their petals. Perhaps from the weight of sprays of up to 20 flowers each, plants have

'spice drop'

a cascading quality that makes them naturals for hanging baskets and for budding as Tree roses. Foliage is small, deep green, and notably disease resistant. (M)

'TEXAS' may not be the yellow rose of Texas, but it's unarguably yellow. Blossoms are most often presented in sprays, but individual flowers have fine form. Plants are upright and vigorous, at their best in cool climates. (T)

'TINY FLAME' is another Micro-mini from the imminently capable hybridizer Ralph Moore. Its coral-red buds and flowers are tiny indeed, as is the plant, which doesn't grow taller than 6 inches. Foliage is small, too, but plants are bushy. (L)

'TOM THUMB', originally named 'Peon', renamed in 1936, and the first Miniature rose introduced to commerce in the United States, remains one of the finest of all Micro-minis. Tiny buds open into 1-inch red flowers with a bright white eye. Even when grown to perfection, mature plants never reach more than 6 inches in height. Foliage is also small but is dense and leathery. (L)

'TRINKET' is yet another Ralph Moore Micro-mini, but one of distinctive coloring— phlox pink. Foliage is small but glossy, and although plants are dwarf, they're vigorous and bushy. (L)

'WINSOME' produces buds that are dark purple, maturing into magenta-and-lavender blossoms of up to 40 petals each. Plants are free flowering and vigorous and naturally grow as well-rounded bushes. Foliage is resistant to disease. (T)

'winsome'

APPENDIX A

American Rose Society
Awards of Excellence for Miniature Roses

1975

'Beauty Secret'
'Judy Fischer'
'Lavender Lace'
'Magic Carrousel'
'Mary Marshall'
'Over the Rainbow'
'Sheri Anne'
'Starglo'
'Toy Clown'
'White Angel'

1976

'Hula Girl'
'Peachy White'
'Red Cascade'

1977

'Jeanne LaJoie'
'Peaches 'n' Cream'

1978

'Avandel'
'Gloriglo'
'Humdinger'
'Rise 'n' Shine'

1 9 7 9
'Cuddles'
'Puppy Love'
'Red Flush'
'Zinger'

1 9 8 0
'Holy Toledo'
'Pink Petticoat'

1 9 8 1
'Pacesetter'
'Party Girl'

1 9 8 2
'Center Gold'

1 9 8 3
'Cornsilk'
'Cupcake'
'Hombre'
'Snow Bride'
'Valerie Jeanne'

1 9 8 4
'Baby Eclipse'
'Hot Shot'
'Julie Ann'
'Little Jackie'

1 9 8 5
'Black Jade'
'Centerpiece'
'Jennifer'
'Loving Touch'
'Winsome'

1 9 8 6
'Jean Kenneally'
'Rainbow's End'

1 9 8 7
'Ring of Fire'
'Sequoia Gold'

1 9 8 8
'Heavenly Days'
'Old Glory'

1 9 8 9
'Dee Bennett'
'Jim Dandy'
'Nighthawk'
'Tipper'

1 9 9 0
'Regine'

A P P E N D I X   A

1   9   9   2
'Cal Poly'
'Debidue'
'Figurine'
'Sincerely Yours'

1   9   9   3
'Billie Teas'
'Boomerang'
'Child's Play'
'Kristen'
'Palmetto Sunrise'

1   9   9   4
'Hot Tamale'

1   9   9   5
'Jingle Bells'

1   9   9   6
'Angelica Renae'

1   9   9   7
'Tropical Twist'

1   9   9   8
'Playgold'

M a i l - O r d e r M i n i a t u r e R o s e S p e c i a l i s t s

Bridges Roses
2734 Toney Road
Lawndale, NC 28090
(704) 538-9412
Fax (704) 538-1521

Michigan Miniature Roses
45951 Hull Road
Belleville, MI 48111
(313) 699-6698
Fax (313) 699-5814

Nor'East Miniature Roses
P.O. Box 307
58 Hammond Street
Rowley, MA 01969
(508) 948-7964
(800) 426-6485
Fax (508) 948-5487
or
P.O. Box 473
Ontario, CA 91762
(909) 984-2223
(800) 662-9669
Fax (909) 986-9875

Pixie Treasures
4121 Prospect Avenue
Yorba Linda, CA 92686
(714) 993-6780

Sequoia Nursery
2519 E. Noble Avenue
Visalia, CA 93292
(209) 732-0190
(Specializing in Ralph Moore varieties)

Taylor's Roses
Nursery: 8450 Gayfer Avenue
Fairhope, AL 36532
(334) 928-5008
Mailing Address: P.O. Box 677
Fairhope, AL 36533

Tiny Petals Nursery
489 Milnot Avenue
Chula Vista, CA 91910
Office/Fax (619) 422-0385
Nursery (619) 498-4755

I N D E X